INTO SPACE

Leon

Hetty

Professor
Verne

Brigit

Toosant

Newton

Headway · Hodder & Stoughton

In the nineteenth century Jules Verne, the famous author, wrote exciting books about journeys of adventure. Now his namesake, Professor Bartholemew Verne, has invented an amazing machine. In it he can follow the journeys Jules Verne wrote about. With his crew of children, he can explore the wonders of the world and of outer space.

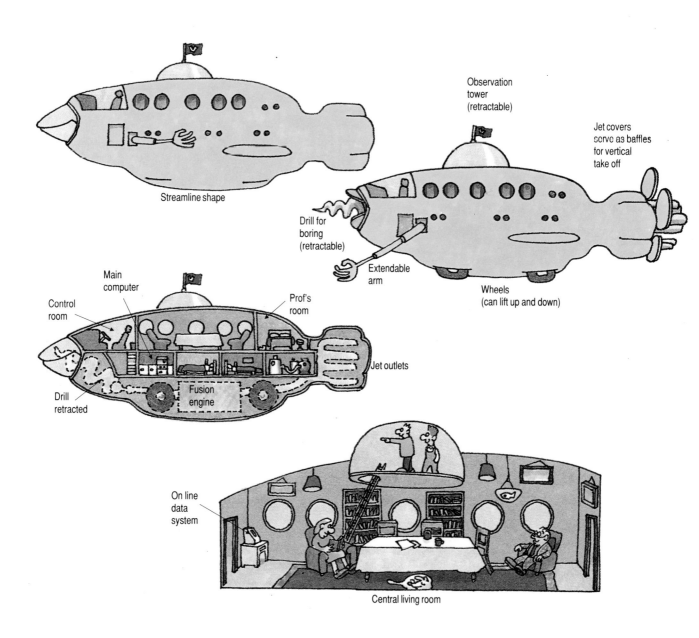

Streamline shape

Observation tower (retractable)

Jet covers serve as baffles for vertical take off

Drill for boring (retractable)

Extendable arm

Wheels (can lift up and down)

Main computer

Control room

Prof's room

Jet outlets

Drill retracted

Fusion engine

On line data system

Central living room

BLAST OFF!

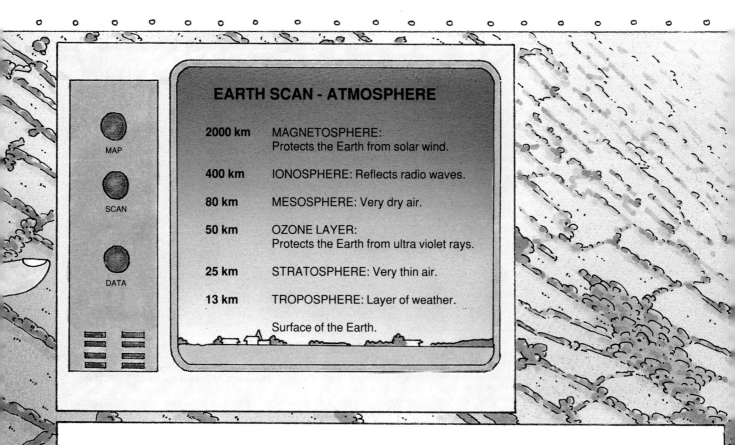

EARTH SCAN - ATMOSPHERE

2000 km	MAGNETOSPHERE: Protects the Earth from solar wind.
400 km	IONOSPHERE: Reflects radio waves.
80 km	MESOSPHERE: Very dry air.
50 km	OZONE LAYER: Protects the Earth from ultra violet rays.
25 km	STRATOSPHERE: Very thin air.
13 km	TROPOSPHERE: Layer of weather.
	Surface of the Earth.

MAP

SCAN

DATA

A thin layer of gas covers the Earth. This is called the *atmosphere*. The atmosphere is at its most dense near to the Earth. Further out it grows thinner and thinner. In outer space there is no atmosphere at all.

The atmosphere is held round the Earth by the force of gravity. This is the same force that makes things fall to Earth if you drop them. To escape from Earth's gravity a spaceship must reach the speed of 11.2 km per second. That's 25,200 miles per hour.

Once in outer space a spaceship can float for ever without falling back to Earth.

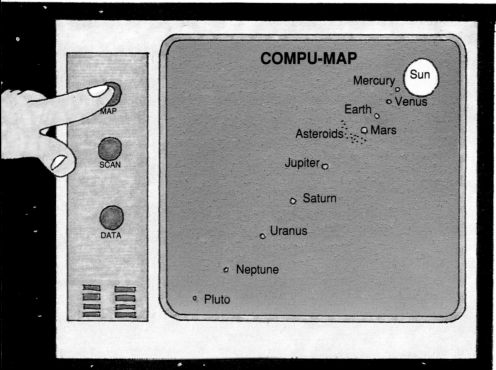

COMPU-MAP

MAP

SCAN

DATA

Mercury
Sun
Venus
Earth
Asteroids
Mars
Jupiter
Saturn
Uranus
Neptune
Pluto

Planet Earth is the only planet which supports life. It is the third planet out from the Sun. At this distance the Sun's heat keeps water liquid. Water makes life possible. Most water on Earth does not freeze into ice or boil into steam. Ninety-seven percent of the water collects in the sea. Seventy-one percent of Earth's surface is covered in water.

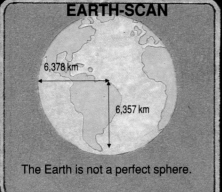

EARTH-SCAN

6,378 km

6,357 km

The Earth is not a perfect sphere.

What does orbit mean?

To travel in a circle round something.

That's what we'll be doing if you don't steer properly!

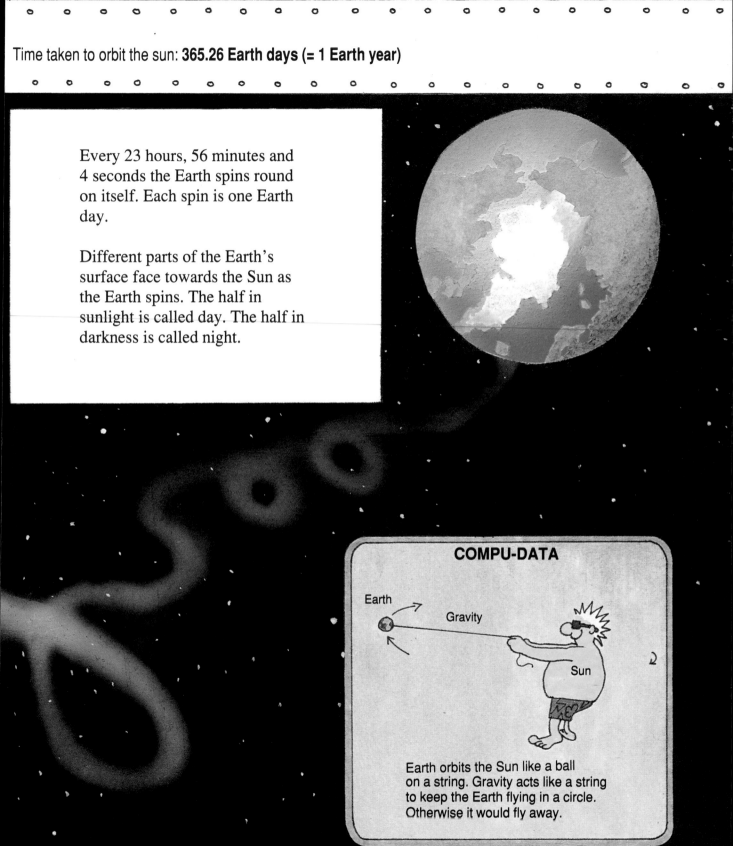

Every 23 hours, 56 minutes and 4 seconds the Earth spins round on itself. Each spin is one Earth day.

Different parts of the Earth's surface face towards the Sun as the Earth spins. The half in sunlight is called day. The half in darkness is called night.

COMPU-DATA

Earth

Gravity

Sun

Earth orbits the Sun like a ball on a string. Gravity acts like a string to keep the Earth flying in a circle. Otherwise it would fly away.

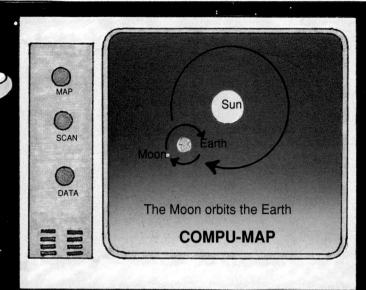

The Moon is Earth's nearest neighbour in space. Although the Moon shines silver at night, this is not its own light. It reflects sunlight like a mirror.

The surface of the Moon is covered in craters. Craters are caused by rocks, called *meteors*, landing from outer space.

8

The large, light-coloured areas on the surface of the Moon are covered in lava from extinct volcanoes. These areas are called seas. The moon has no atmosphere so the sky stays black even in daylight. There is no sound on the moon because sound cannot travel through empty space.

COMPU-DATA

In July 1969 Neil Armstrong was the first man to step on the Moon. His footsteps will still be in the powdery Moon dust ten million years from now. There is nothing to disturb them!

Extinct volcanoes

9

COMPU-DATA

Sun

Earth

The Sun is much bigger than the Earth.

MAP

SCAN

DATA

The Sun is a star. The Sun and its planets are called the *Solar System*. Solar means 'of the Sun'. All the planets in the Solar System orbit the Sun, which is bigger than all of them put together.

The Sun is a ball of incredibly hot gas. Its centre is like a huge hydrogen bomb which never stops exploding. Light from its surface takes 8.3 minutes to reach the Earth.

There are patches of cooler gas on its surface. These are called sunspots. It is thought that sunspots affect the Earth's climate.

Approximate age: **4,600 million Earth years**
Temperature: **14 million degrees centigrade at the core; 5,500 degrees centigrade at the surface**

Our jet trail's blowing away from the Sun!

It's being blown by the solar wind!

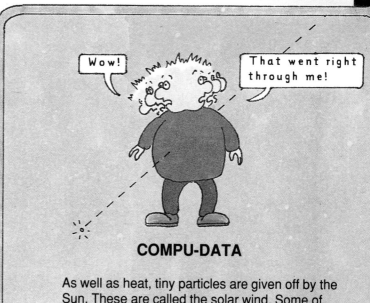

Wow!

That went right through me!

COMPU-DATA

As well as heat, tiny particles are given off by the Sun. These are called the solar wind. Some of these particles are so small that 100 million pass right through the Earth and out the other side every second, without touching anything!

Destination: # MERCURY

Distance from the Sun: **57,895,200 km**

Time to orbit the Sun: **87.969 Earth days**
Temperature: **Day 350 °C**
Temperature: **Night 170 °C**
Radius: **2,439 km**

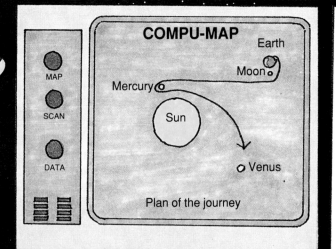

COMPU-MAP

MAP

SCAN

DATA

Earth
Moon
Mercury
Sun
Venus

Plan of the journey

Mercury is the closest planet to the Sun. It is not much larger than the Moon, but is much heavier. This is probably because it contains a lot of iron. Iron is very heavy.

One side of Mercury always faces the Sun. This side becomes very hot. Maximum temperatures are hot enough to melt lead and zinc.

It looks very old and wrinkly.

Planets in the Solar System are the same age as the Sun.

COMPU-DATA

The surface of Mercury is wrinkled like an old apple. The iron in its core has shrunk. So now the surface is too big for the centre.

Destination: **VENUS**
Distance from the Sun: **1,081,160,800 km**

Time to orbit the Sun: **224.7 Earth days**
Surface temperature: **Up to 480 °C**
Radius: **6,052 km**

Venus is the hottest planet in the Solar System, and the second closest to the Sun. The heat of the Sun is trapped by its thick atmosphere. It has pale yellow clouds of concentrated sulphuric acid in its sky. These can reach speeds of 300 km per hour.

Once there were oceans on Venus. These have long since boiled away in the intense heat.

WARNING !!!
VENUS IS
VERY DANGEROUS

**HUMAN LIFE
IMPOSSIBLE**

DO NOT LEAVE THE
SPACE CRAFT

Ugh! It's raining concentrated sulphuric acid!

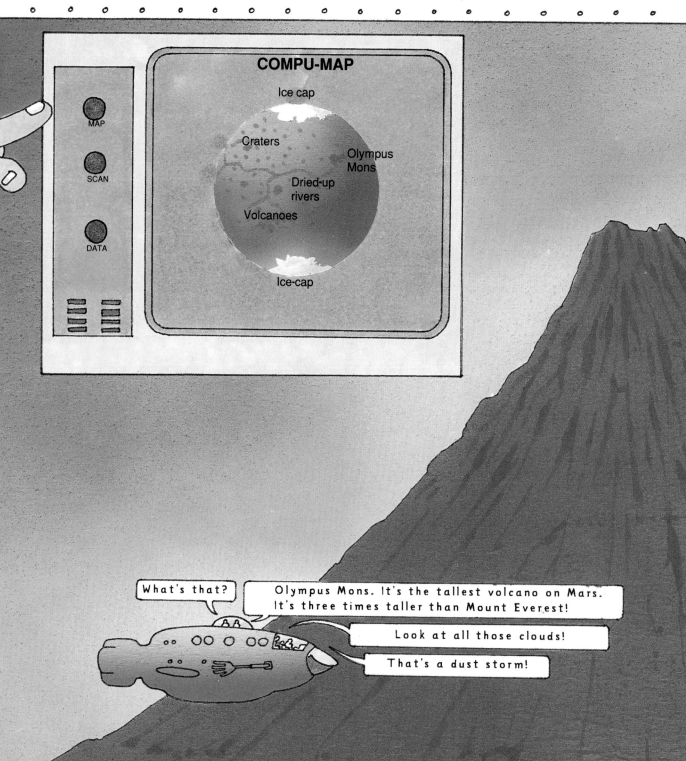

Mars is the fourth planet from the sun. Of all the planets, Mars has conditions most like Earth. It has valleys, plains and giant volcanoes. Mars once had rivers and lakes. The paths of dried-up rivers can still be seen on its surface.

The Martian atmosphere has grown thinner over the centuries. It is now too thin to trap much heat from the Sun. Mars has grown too cold for water to remain liquid. Its water is now frozen in the ground at its north and south poles. The ice-caps are formed from frozen carbon-dioxide.

For many years people hoped to find intelligent life on Mars. This is now thought impossible.

COMPU-DATA

Mars is the name of the Roman god of war. The planet was called Mars because of its blood-red colour. It has two moons: one called Phobos, which means fear, and the other Deimos, meaning terror.

COMPU-MAP

Sun
Mercury
Venus
Earth
Mars
Asteroids
Jupiter

MAP
SCAN
DATA

Wow! That asteroid looks like a cauliflower!

Asteroids have irregular shapes.

Estimated numbers: **There are over 1 billion asteroids**
More than 500,000 are longer than 1 km

Most asteroids circle the Sun between the orbits of Mars and Jupiter. They are sometimes known as the Minor Planets. This region of the Solar System is called the *Asteroid Belt*.

Asteroids vary in size from a few centimetres to several kilometres across. Ceres, the largest-known asteroid, is 512 km long. About 40,000 tonnes of asteroids hit Earth's atmosphere every year. Two hundred tonnes reach the ground. These are called *meteorites*.

COMPU-DATA

A major asteroid collides with Earth at least once every million years. It is thought that changes to the Earth's climate, as a result of an asteroid collision, may have caused the extinction of the dinosaurs.

Destination: **JUPITER**
Distance from the Sun: **778 million km**

Time to orbit the Sun: **4,329 Earth days**
Surface temperature: **-150°C**
Radius: **71,492 km**
Satellites: **1**

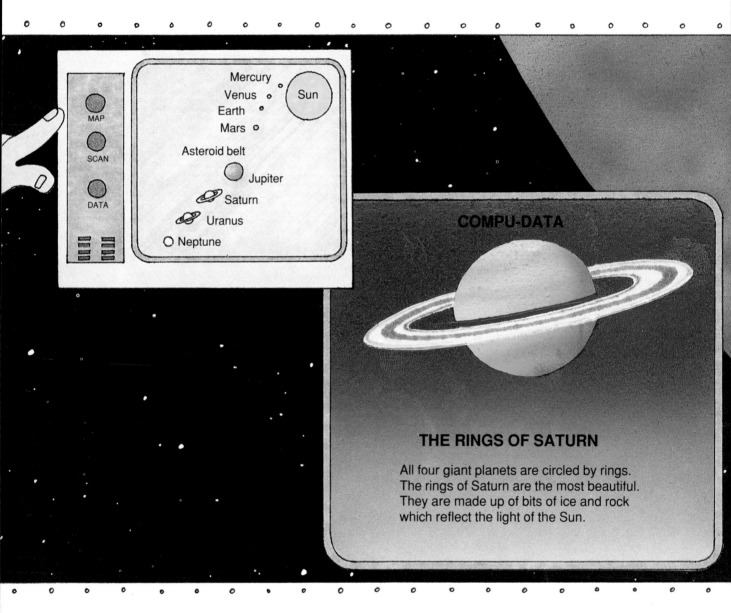

Mercury
Venus
Earth
Mars
Asteroid belt
Sun
Jupiter
Saturn
Uranus
Neptune

MAP
SCAN
DATA

COMPU-DATA

THE RINGS OF SATURN

All four giant planets are circled by rings.
The rings of Saturn are the most beautiful.
They are made up of bits of ice and rock
which reflect the light of the Sun.

Destination: **URANUS**
Distance from the Sun: **3,774 million km**

Time to orbit the Sun: **84 Earth years**
Surface temperature: **-210°C**
Radius: **25,359 km**
Known satellites: **15**

Destination: **SATURN**

Distance from the Sun: 1,427 million km

Time to orbit the Sun: **10,752 Earth days**
Surface temperature: **-180°C**
Radius: **60,330 km**
Satellites: **17**

Four giant planets circle the Sun beyond the Asteroid Belt.
They are much larger than the inner planets. Jupiter is the
largest. It is larger than all the other planets put together.
It is so large that a thousand Earths could fit inside it.
None of the planets support life, as far as we know.

What's that bad smell?

That's Jupiter's atmosphere.
The smell is from ammonia
and hydrogen sulphide.

Atmosphere sample scoop

Destination: **NEPTUNE**

Distance from the Sun: 4,503 million km

Time to orbit the Sun: **165 Earth years**
Surface temperature: **-220°C**
Radius: **24,760 km**
Satellites: **8**

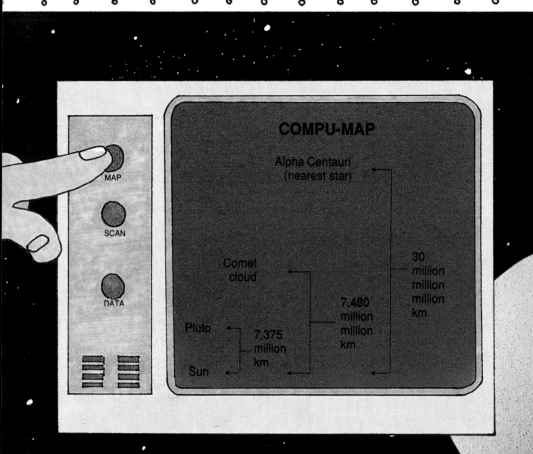

COMPU-MAP

MAP

SCAN

DATA

Alpha Centauri
(nearest star)

Comet
cloud

30
million
million
million
km

7,480
million
million
km

Pluto

7,375
million
km

Sun

Wow! Look at that
giant snowball!

That's Pluto. It's the coldest
planet. It's made of rock and ice.

Pluto is usually the last planet in the solar system. Sometimes Neptune passes it. Pluto is also the smallest planet. In fact, it's smaller than the Moon. But Pluto is not the last object in the Solar System. The comets circle the Sun at much greater distances.

Comets are lumps of rock and ice. At their furthest, they can travel a quarter of the way to the nearest star. But some also approach so close to the heat of the Sun that they grow huge tails, up to 100 million km long. These tails are made up of water and dust. Comets can give off millions of tons of water and dust every day. We sometimes see their tails in the night sky.

COMPU-DATA

Comet dust can be so small that it enters the Earth's atmosphere without burning up. You've probably got some comet dust in your hair right now!

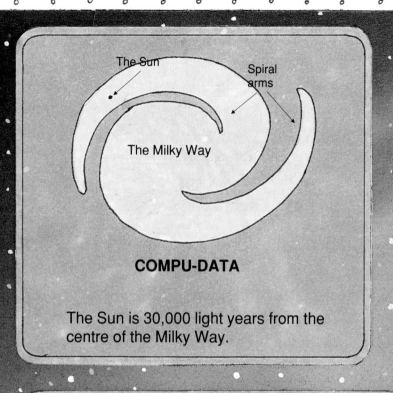

COMPU-DATA

The Sun is 30,000 light years from the centre of the Milky Way.

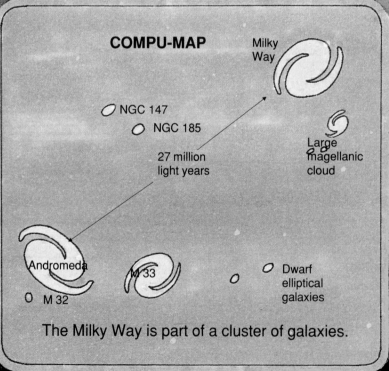

COMPU-MAP

The Milky Way is part of a cluster of galaxies.

Period of time taken to spin round on itself: **200 million years**
Number of stars: **100 billion**

So this is the Milky Way.

It's not really milk. It's our galaxy.

There must be a very large cow round here.

Wow!

COMPU-DATA

A light year is the distance light travels in one year. Light travels at a speed of 300,000 km per hour. So one light year is 2,628,000,000 km long.

Galaxies are clusters of millions of stars. Our star, the Sun, is part of a galaxy called the Milky Way. There are a hundred billion other stars in the Milky Way. Galaxies like ours are called *spiral galaxies* because they have spiral arms. New stars are formed in the spiral arms. The Sun is a medium-sized star in one of the spiral arms.

Other galaxies circle round the Milky Way. The nearest of these is the *Large Magellanic Cloud*. It is 180,000 light years away.

Destination: **BLACK HOLE**

Scientists know that the centre of the Milky Way is as heavy as 5 million stars.

Some objects in space become too heavy for themselves. The heavier an object, the stronger its gravity. These objects are squeezed towards their own centres by the force of their own gravity. They grow heavier still as they grow smaller. Eventually they collapse into a *black hole*. They are called black holes because their gravity is so strong that nothing, not even light, can escape them.

So when we look at them, we see black nothingness. Some black holes are millions of light years across, some only a few kilometres across. There are probably black holes all over the universe.

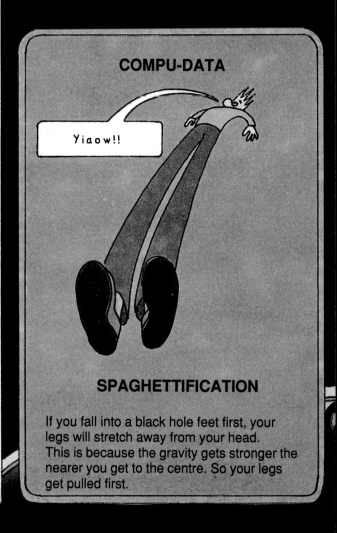

COMPU-DATA

Yiaow!!

SPAGHETTIFICATION

If you fall into a black hole feet first, your legs will stretch away from your head. This is because the gravity gets stronger the nearer you get to the centre. So your legs get pulled first.

ut there are only about 1 million stars at the centre. **Where are the missing stars?**
hey have probably shrunk into an enormous black hole...

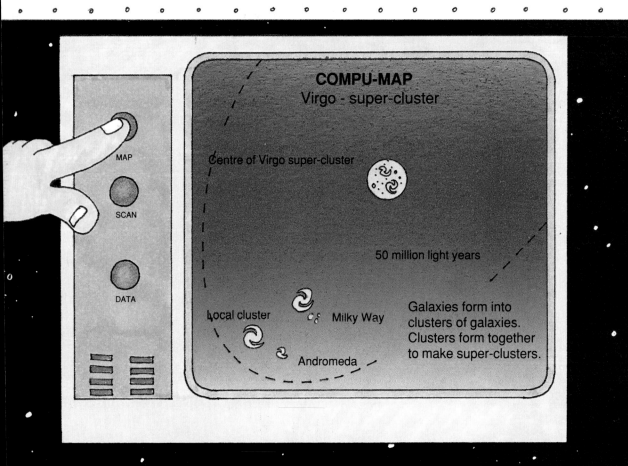

COMPU-MAP
Virgo - super-cluster

Centre of Virgo super-cluster

50 million light years

Local cluster   Milky Way

Andromeda

Galaxies form into clusters of galaxies. Clusters form together to make super-clusters.

MAP

SCAN

DATA

The Milky Way is just one of billions of galaxies in the universe. Scientists have discovered that all the galaxies are moving away from each other. Long ago they were much closer together. In fact, scientists think that everything in the universe exploded outwards from a tiny dot, probably about 15,000 million years ago. This is known as the *Big Bang theory*.

With powerful telescopes, we can see very distant bright objects called *Quasars*. The furthest object we can see is 12,000 million light years away. That means that the light from this distant quasar started its journey to our eyes 12,000 million years ago. When we look at it, we are looking at a time only 3,000 million years after the start of the universe!

COMPU-DATA

Many scientists think that Quasars are the incredibly bright centres of some very distant galaxies. Some Quasars are brighter than 10 million million Suns. That's why we can see them from so far away.

Life as we know it is made of water and compounds of carbon. All living cells on Earth are two-thirds water. To support life, plants will need to contain liquid water. Scientists think there may be a billion such planets in our galaxy which are capable of supporting life.

It is very unlikely that we are alone in the universe. Some life forms may be different to those we know on Earth. One scientist has suggested that huge gas-bag fish may be swimming in a layer of liquid water on Jupiter.

COMPU-DATA

Distances between the stars are so great that we may never meet other life. It would take 80,000 years for a space probe just to reach the nearest star, with present technology. That's more than a thousand lifetimes!

Number of planets in the universe which could support life: **Possibly billions**

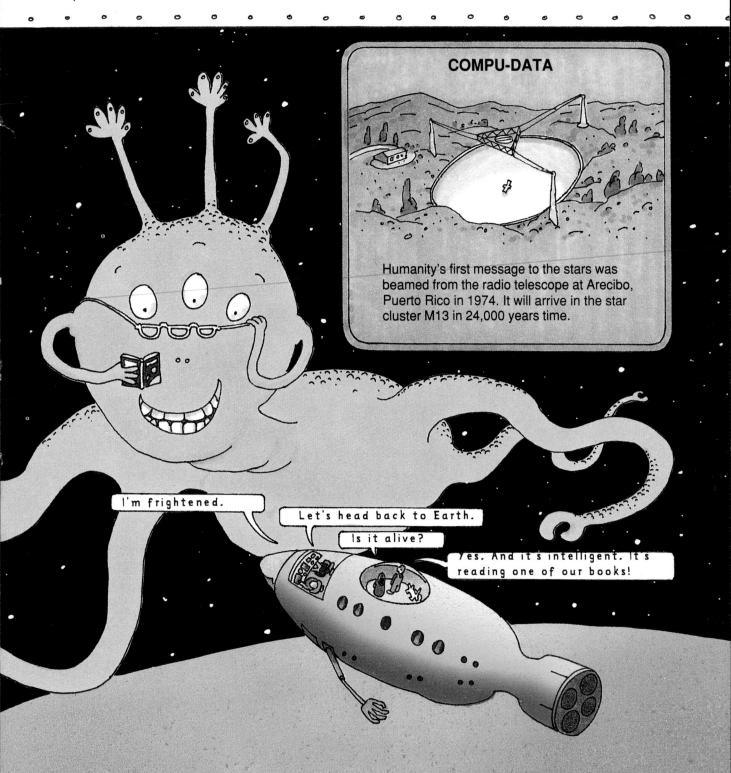

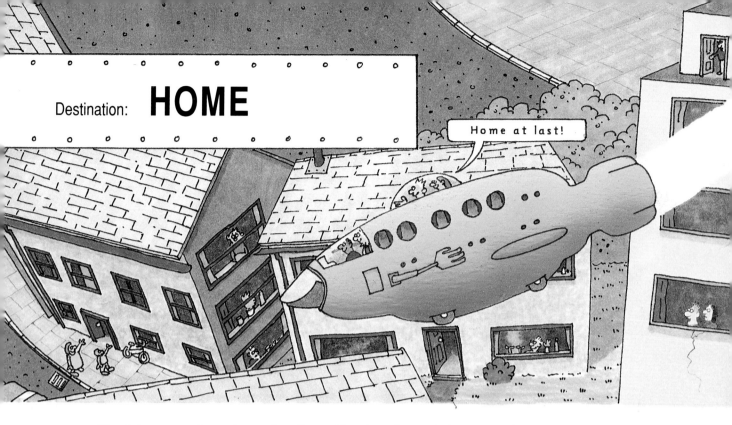

Destination: **HOME**

Home at last!

Earth's atmosphere is made of gas. Passing through it at speed causes heat and friction. Objects like meteors and spacecraft can burn up when they enter Earth's atmosphere. Spacecraft must protect their nose cones with a thick shield of heat-resistant material.

GLOSSARY

Atmosphere is the layer of gases surrounding planets.

Black hole is an object in space with such massive gravity that light cannot escape.

Comets are objects usually moving in a very long and thin orbit of the sun.

Cosmic dust is made from small particles in or from outer space.

Galaxies are irregular bands of many millions of stars held together by the force of gravity.

Quasars appear like a star but give off more light than several hundred giant galaxies.

Solar system includes the sun and all the planets and objects bound to it by gravity.

Solar wind is made from tiny charged particles which flow out from the sun into space.

Now that you've found out all about space, let's see how much you can remember.

Professor Verne's *Outer Space* quiz

1. *What is a radius*?
   a) nuclear waste
   b) the distance from the centre to the edge of a circle
   c) a charm

2. *Who was Neil Armstrong?*
   a) a champion boxer
   b) the first man on the moon
   c) a trumpet player

3. *What are asteroids?*
   a) a nasty disease
   b) pieces of rock in space
   c) punctuation marks

4. *What is a quasar?*
   a) the heir to the throne of Russia
   b) an exploding galaxy
   c) a sick feeling

5. *What is the solar system*
   a) a type of central heating
   b) a roundabout
   c) the Sun and its planets

6. *What are the rings of Saturn?*
   a) a type of jewellery
   b) a chime of bells
   c) rings of ice and dust round Saturn

Answers: 1) b.   2) b.   3) b.   4) b.   5) c.   6) c.

INDEX

British Library Cataloguing in Publication Data
Johnson, Kipchak
  Into Space. - (Fantastic Journey Series)
  I. Title II. Series
  520
ISBN 0 340 57083 0
First published 1992
© 1992 Kipchak Johnson/Lazy Summer Books

The rights of Kipchak Johnson to be identified as the author of the text
of this work has been asserted by him in accordance with the Copyright,
Designs and Patents Act 1988.

Printed in Great Britain for the educational publishing division of
Hodder and Stoughton Ltd, Mill Road, Dunton Green, Sevenoaks, Kent
by Cambus Litho Limited, East Kilbride.